YOUR SYSTEMATIC PATH TO FINANCIAL FREEDOM

Mutual Funds made simple - SIP your way in, SWP your way out.

NIHAL KASHINATH KIRNALLI

Made with ♥ on the Notion Press Platform

www.notionpress.com

To

every hardworking individual

who dreams of a financially secure and peaceful life,

yet wonders where to begin...

To the everyday earners who believe wealth is only for the rich — this is for you.

And to my family, mentors, and clients

whose trust, support, and questions

inspired every word of this book.

May this guide help you build wealth,

not just for yourself, but for generations to come.

Contents

Foreword

In a world full of financial noise and short-term temptations, the true art of wealth-building lies in simplicity, consistency, and discipline. Your Systematic Path to Financial Freedom brings that clarity in a language that is practical, relatable, and deeply impactful.

Having worked in the financial services industry for over a decade, I have witnessed first-hand the transformation that occurs when individuals shift from unstructured savings to well-planned, goal-based investing. The tools are already within reach—Mutual Funds, SIPs, and SWPs—but what's often missing is the guidance to use them wisely. This book fills that gap.

Nihal has taken a complex subject and presented it with both heart and logic. With relatable examples, step-by-step approaches, and a genuine desire to help the everyday Indian become financially independent, this book is more than just a guide—it's a movement.

What I admire most is the way Nihal connects with readers, not as a financial expert preaching from above, but as a friend walking alongside. Whether you're just starting your financial journey or looking to retire with dignity and abundance, this book will be your companion.

I strongly recommend you not just read this book—but act on it. Your future self will thank you.

Samadhan Mane
Branch Manager,
NJ Wealth India Pvt. Ltd.,
SOLAPUR Branch.

Preface

Why This Book Exists

In every corner of India, you'll find someone working tirelessly, saving carefully, and still worrying endlessly about the future. I've met hundreds of them — school teachers, shop owners, government officers, IT employees and even high-earning professionals — all stuck in the same race: earn, spend, save a little, repeat.

What if I told you there's a better way?

Not a shortcut. Not a scam. But a system — silent, steady, and smart — that's been changing lives for decades. It's called Mutual Funds. This book isn't just about jargon or charts, It's about choices.

The choice to take control of your money.

The choice to build wealth without sacrificing your life for it.

The choice to leave behind a legacy, not just bills.

This is not a financial textbook. It's a guide. A mirror. And sometimes, a wake-up call. You'll find stories, numbers, strategies — all woven together to help you make one powerful shift:

> From earning wages to creating wealth.

Let's begin your journey from worry… to wealth.

— Nihal Kashinath Kirnalli

Acknowledgements

Writing this book has been a fulfilling journey, and I would not have completed it without the support, encouragement, and inspiration of many individuals.

First and foremost, I express my heartfelt gratitude to my clients, whose trust and belief in me as a financial guide continue to motivate me every single day. Their questions, experiences, and aspirations shaped the real essence of this book.

I am deeply thankful to my family, whose unwavering support, patience, and love gave me the strength to pursue this project. Your belief in my vision means more than words can express.

To my mentors and senior advisors in the financial industry — thank you for your wisdom, guidance, and constant encouragement to share knowledge with a broader audience.

Special thanks to my friends and well-wishers, who offered valuable feedback, encouragement, and ideas during the writing process.

Lastly, I want to thank every individual who believes in Mutual Funds and is taking the Systematic Path to Financial Freedom through disciplined SIPs and wise SWPs. This book is for you.

May this work inspire you to take control of your finances and build wealth that lasts generations.

With gratitude,

Nihal Kashinath Kirnalli

Prologue

We all dream of living a life free from financial stress — a life where money is no longer a daily worry but a tool to fulfil our purpose, take care of our loved ones, and enjoy the freedom we truly deserve.

But for most people, financial freedom feels distant. The world of investing can appear complex, risky, or only meant for the wealthy. This belief holds millions back from taking that one simple step — starting a systematic plan.

I have seen countless individuals with average incomes create extraordinary financial stability — not through luck or shortcuts, but through SIPs, Mutual Funds, and smart planning. I have also seen people with large incomes fall into financial traps due to poor money habits and lack of direction.

This book is born out of real-life conversations, questions, and the common struggles people face when it comes to managing money. It's written not as a textbook, but as a friend's advice — practical, simple, and actionable.

In the pages ahead, you will discover how Systematic Investment Plans (SIPs) can help you accumulate wealth, and how Systematic Withdrawal Plans (SWPs) can help you enjoy that wealth with dignity. More importantly, you'll understand how small, consistent actions can lead to massive financial transformation.

This is not just a book about money — it's about mindset, discipline, and freedom.

Welcome to your journey.

Let's walk this path — systematically.

— Nihal Kirnalli

1

Your WHY

The Day I Met Someone Just Like You…

A few years ago, I was sitting across the table from a 42-year-old government officer. Let's call him Mr. Patil. He had a decent salary, two children, and a wife who worked part-time. He told me proudly that he had saved ₹15 lakhs in FDs and owned a small flat in Solapur.

I asked him just one question:

"What's your plan if your salary stops tomorrow?"

There was silence.

Then came a half-smile. "I'll manage somehow. I've always managed."

But have we?

Have you?

Like Mr. Patil, most of us don't have a financial plan. We have habits. We follow what our parents did: put money in FDs, buy property, wait, and hope. But hope is not a financial strategy.

The Power of a Clear WHY

We often underestimate the silent thief that erodes our wealth every single year — **inflation**. It doesn't make headlines every day, but it affects every rupee you spend. Think about this: in 2012, a litre of milk cost around ₹20, but by 2025, it's touching around ₹60 — that's a 200% jump in just over a decade. Consider petrol: the average price in 2012 was approximately ₹68.57 per litre, and by 2024, it had climbed to about ₹100 per litre.

This means your everyday expenses keep rising, while traditional savings such as gold and real estate might only grow slowly and provide you a hedge against inflation. If your money isn't growing faster than inflation, you're not just standing still — you're falling behind. That's why a systematic investing strategy isn't just smart, it's essential for preserving and growing your investments over time.

Now imagine this — you have ₹1,00,000 today and you decide to keep it idle, not even in a savings account. It feels safe, right? But what most people don't realize is that inflation quietly eats into its value every single year. If inflation averages just 6% per year, then after 10 years, your ₹1,00,000 will have the purchasing power of barely ₹53,000.

In simple words, you'll lose almost half your money's worth — without ever spending a rupee. That's the danger of keeping money idle. It's not just about growing your wealth, it's also about protecting it from silently shrinking. And that's exactly why investing systematically becomes not just smart — but necessary.

The Saving Illusion

Most people say,

"I'm saving ₹5,000 every month."

Great. But where?

"FDs? Savings Account?"

Let's do the math:

- Average FD return (post tax): ~5%
- Average inflation in India: ~6%

So even though your money looks safe in the bank, it's actually shrinking in value.

That's like putting your money in a locker that leaks.

What Happens Over Time?

Let's say you save ₹10 lakhs in FDs for 20 years at 5% return.

- You'll get around ₹26.5 lakhs.
- But with 7% inflation, that ₹26.5 lakhs will have the buying power of just ₹6.8 lakhs today.

You didn't grow your money. You just preserved a part of it.

The Investor's Advantage

Now imagine the same ₹10 lakh invested in Mutual Funds with 12% average returns over 20 years.

- Final corpus: ₹96.5 lakhs+
- Adjusted for 7% inflation: worth ~₹25 lakhs in today's value.

Even after inflation, you've grown your money nearly 2.5X in real terms.

That's the difference between saving and investing.

Saving protects money. Investing multiplies it.

Your journey to wealth won't begin with numbers. It begins with clarity.

Ask yourself:

- Do I want to stop worrying about money?
- Do I want to retire without depending on my children?
- Do I want to give my kids a better future without loans?
- Do I want to be rich, not just look rich?

If your answer is "Yes" to even one… you already have your WHY.

Now all you need is the HOW.

And that's exactly what this book will give you.

Let's move ahead.

2

The Money Trap

Why Most People Struggle Financially, Even If They Work Hard?

Let me tell you about Ravi — a software engineer in Mumbai, earning ₹18 lakhs a year.

By all external measures, Ravi was "doing well." He drove a car with EMI, lived in a rented 2BHK flat in Powai, and went on two vacations a year. On paper, his life was perfect.

But inside, Ravi was anxious.

Every month, his salary disappeared. EMIs, school fees, dining out, credit card bills… poof. When his father needed a ₹2 lakh surgery, Ravi had to borrow from a friend. Despite earning ₹1.5 lakh per month, Ravi couldn't handle an emergency.

Ravi wasn't alone.

He was trapped — just like millions of others - in the Money Trap.

What is the Money Trap?

It's the silent cycle that looks like this:

Earn → Spend → Pay EMI → Barely Save → Repeat

This trap doesn't care about how much you earn. Whether it's ₹30,000 or ₹3,00,000 per month — if you don't control your money, your money will control you.

The trap is invisible because it feels normal.

Society celebrates spending. Banks offer easy EMIs. Social media pressurizes you to "look successful." No one teaches us to be financially free. They only teach us to earn more.

But here's the truth:

Earning more doesn't make you rich. Managing what you earn does.

The money trap is the cycle where higher income leads to higher expenses, leaving little to no savings despite earning more. It often begins subtly—an upgraded phone here, a bigger car there—justified as "rewards" for hard work. Over time, lifestyle inflation consumes potential investments, trapping people in a pay cheque-to-pay cheque routine even at high salaries. The real danger is that this trap feels comfortable, making it harder to break free. Escaping it requires conscious discipline: living below your means, prioritizing savings and investments, and remembering that wealth is built not by what you earn, but by what you keep and grow.

The Illusion of Growth

Ravi got a promotion. His salary went up. But so did his lifestyle.

Better phone. Bigger car. Nicer clothes.

But not one rupee extra went into wealth creation.

This is called Lifestyle Inflation.

And it's the reason why people retire poor even after earning well their entire lives.

Let me ask you something:

- What will your FD give you in 20 years?
- Is your money growing faster than inflation?
- If you stop working tomorrow, how many months can you survive?

If these questions made you uncomfortable — good.

That means you're awake now.

How Do You Escape the Trap?

You need a new path. Not more work. Not another side hustle.

You need a system that works quietly in the background, every single month, growing your wealth like a silent business partner.

That system is Mutual Funds.

And more importantly, the habit that powers it is Systematic Investment Plans (SIP).

We'll get to that very soon.

But before we do, let's understand the magic that makes all of this possible — a force so powerful it's been called the eighth wonder of the world by none other than Mr. Albert Einstein.

Let's talk about Compounding.

3

The Power of Compounding

The Silent Force That Builds Wealth While You Sleep

There's an old story I often share in my presentations. It goes like this:

A wise king once told a farmer,

"I'll reward you. Ask for anything."

The farmer said,

"Place one grain of rice on the first square of a chessboard, and double it on every square."

The king laughed. "That's it?"

He ordered the grains to be placed.

1… 2… 4… 8… 16…

By the 30th square, the palace ran out of rice.

By the 64th square, the king owed more rice than existed on Earth.

That's Compounding.

It looks slow in the beginning. Almost boring. But with time — it explodes.

The Simple Math Behind the Magic

Let's talk real money now.

Suppose you start investing ₹5,000/month via SIP at 12% annual return:

Years	Total Invested	Corpus Value
5	₹ 3,00,000	₹ 4,05,000
10	₹ 6,00,000	₹ 11,20,000
15	₹ 9,00,000	₹ 23,80,000
20	₹ 12,00,000	₹ 46,00,000
25	₹ 15,00,000	₹ 85,11,000
30	₹ 18,00,000	₹ 1,54,00,000

The Power of Compounding

By year 5, you won't see much monetary gain in your portfolio. Add another 5 years, and you'll start seeing glimpses of the power we call compounding. By 30 years, your ₹18 lakh investment can grow into a humongous ₹1.54 crore!

Let that sink in: **₹18 Lakhs invested → ₹1.65 Crores created.**

Just by being consistent and patient.

Time is the Secret Ingredient. Compounding doesn't reward intelligence. It rewards patience and discipline.

The sooner you start; the more time your money gets to multiply.

Here's a simple story:

- Amit starts SIP of ₹5,000/month at age 25 and stops at 35. (Invested for only 10 Years)

- Rohit starts the same SIP at 35 and continues till 60. (Invested for 25 Years)

Guess who ends up with more money at age 60?

Amit does!

Even though he invested for only 10 years.

That's because time > money when it comes to compounding.

Why Most People Miss This

We live in a world of instant gratification.

10-minutes delivery. 15-second reels. Flash sales.

We want results — now.

But wealth doesn't work like that.

Wealth is built slowly. Silently. Systematically.

These days, many people are drawn to options trading because of the thrill — watching an option premium jump from ₹5 to ₹100 within minutes can be exciting. But the real question is: does this truly help in building sustainable wealth?

Regulatory changes are a constant challenge. SEBI frequently issues new circulars affecting retail trading. For example, daily expiry option contracts were introduced, only to be withdrawn within a year. As of August 2025, there's even talks of weekly option contracts being discontinued.

Clearly, regulatory risk is a significant hurdle in the Options & Futures market in India. While a trader might have one exceptional year, achieving consistent positive returns — let alone a 15% CAGR — over the long term is extremely difficult.

SEBI data shows that more than 90% of retail traders chasing quick profits or extraordinary returns end up making losses, far from achieving even modest compounding.

Add to this the enormous time commitment, the constant monitoring, and the emotional strain of losing streaks. The effort often outweighs the reward. In comparison, Mutual Funds can provide a steady 12% — and in some cases even 15% — CAGR, with minimal human intervention, far less stress, and a far more predictable path to wealth creation.

"If you're not getting rich slowly, you're not getting rich at all."

In Mutual Funds, most people give up too soon — just before compounding starts to show its magic.

Don't make that mistake. Let's understand why is it important for us to stay invested for a long term even if our portfolio is negative in the initial 5-6 years!

Let's observe the chart on the next page which shows the performance of the HSBC Value Fund, where an investor started a Systematic Investment Plan (SIP) of ₹5,000 per month from January 1, 2014. Each row captures the investment value and returns at different points in time.

HSBC Value Fund SIP : ₹ 5,000 Starting : 01-01-2014				
Date	Invested Amount	Current Value	Net Profit	CAGR % Return
01-01-2015	₹ 60,000	₹ 83,781	₹ 23,781	39.64 %
01-01-2016	₹ 1,20,000	₹ 1,59,506	₹ 39,506	29.98 %
01-01-2017	₹ 1,80,000	₹ 2,36,253	₹ 56,253	18.5 %
01-01-2018	₹ 2,40,000	₹ 4,04,506	₹ 1,64,506	26.77 %
01-01-2019	₹ 3,00,000	₹ 4,21,606	₹ 1,21,606	13.56 %
01-01-2020	₹ 3,60,000	₹ 5,07,066	₹ 1,47,066	11.29 %
23-03-2020	₹ 3,75,000	₹ 3,27,045	₹ -47,952	- 4.36 %
01-01-2021	₹ 4,20,000	₹ 6,66,664	₹ 2,46,664	12.95 %
01-01-2022	₹ 4,80,000	₹ 10,10,818	₹ 5,30,818	18.09 %
01-01-2023	₹ 5,40,000	₹ 11,38,781	₹ 5,98,781	15.98 %
01-01-2024	₹ 6,00,000	₹ 16,83,974	₹ 10,83,974	19.58 %
01-01-2025	₹ 6,60,000	₹ 22,07,353	₹ 15,47,353	20.55 %

YOY SIP performance of HSBC Value Fund since January 2014

If you look closely, you'll notice:

In the early years, returns were strong, with double-digit growth—e.g., by January 2015, a ₹60,000 investment had grown to over ₹83,000 (a 39% return).

Over time, the invested amount kept increasing as the SIP continued, building a larger corpus.

On March 23, 2020, during the COVID-19 market crash, the value dropped sharply: ₹3.75 lakh invested was worth only ₹3.27 lakh, showing a negative return of –4.36%.

This moment is critical:

Many investors panic and stop investing when they see negative returns even after six years of disciplined investing. In such times, you'll hear ten different voices telling you that investing in Mutual Funds was a bad decision. Some will even say, "If you had put this money in an FD, it would have been better."

The fear in the atmosphere considering market fall, amplifies the doubt, and without proper guidance — ideally from a Registered Mutual Fund Distributor — more than 90% of investors investing through Direct plans end up booking their losses, never to return to investing again. In doing so, they unknowingly shut the doors to their own Financial Freedom.

However, the data in the table above proves a different story. Investors who stayed patient, continued their SIPs, and trusted the process witnessed a remarkable recovery — a true reward for their perseverance.

By January 2021, the corpus had grown to over ₹6.6 lakh.

By January 2025 (11 Years of Investing), the corpus reached ₹22 lakhs, with a substantial profit of ₹15.47 lakh and a long-term CAGR of over 20%.

This example is based on the HSBC Value Fund. While returns will vary from one fund to another — some may deliver gains of ₹13 lakhs, others ₹14 lakhs — in this case, the gain was ₹15.47 lakhs. Even so, turning an investment of just ₹6.6 lakhs into such substantial growth is undeniably rewarding.

Disclaimer: The above example of HSBC Value Fund provided is solely for educational purpose to illustrate the concept discussed. It should not be construed as a recommendation to invest in the

HSBC Value Fund or any specific mutual fund. Past performance may not be indicative of future results. Investors should consult a qualified financial advisor before making any investment decisions.

Why this data is important:

This data demonstrates why staying invested for the long term is non-negotiable:

Markets move in cycles. Short-term falls—even deep ones—are temporary.

Investors who panic and exit lock in losses permanently.

Those who trust the process and continue their SIPs benefit from recovery and compounding.

In other words, time in the market is more important than timing the market.

Your Job is Simple:

1. Start early.

2. Invest regularly.

3. Stay invested for the long term.

Let your money do the hard work while you live your life.

In the next chapter, we will embark on a journey of perspective and patience. You'll discover how, despite short-term dips and dramatic headlines, the market's long-term trajectory has always pointed upward. By understanding this truth, you'll learn to hold your ground, stay invested, and ride the wave to your financial summit.

4

Trust the Climb – Why Markets Always Rise Over Time

When you look at the Nifty50's monthly chart over the past three decades, one thing becomes clear — the path is never a straight line. There are sharp climbs, sudden drops, and stretches of sideways movement.

Every major fall in the market feels intimidating when you're in it. Headlines scream doom, experts predict deeper crashes, and fear spreads among investors. Yet history repeatedly shows us that every fall is temporary, and each recovery often takes the market to new highs.

Usually, such "red years" last for roughly three years. In your investment journey. And as discussed in earlier chapters — our focus should always remain long term. Even if you encounter two such phases of three-year declines, these should be seen as opportunities rather than threats. Why? Because during such times, your average purchase price for mutual fund units goes down, allowing you to own more units at a lower cost. When the market recovers, these additional units work harder for you, accelerating compounding and boosting your overall returns.

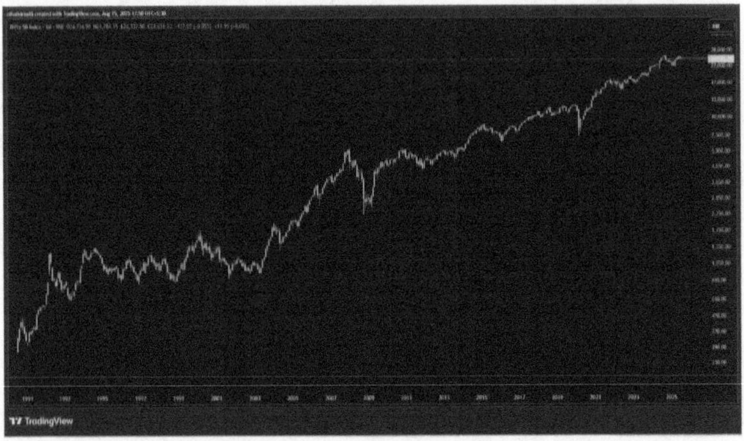

Monthly Chart of the Nifty 50 Index: July 1990 to July 2025

A simple observation of the above chart reveals that since 1990, markets have been steadily climbing at about a 45-degree angle. Let's revisit the major market declines in the last 20 years and see how they eventually turned into opportunities:

1.) 2008 – Global Recession

Fall Duration: 9 months (Jan 2008 – Oct 2008)

% Fall: -59%

Recovery Duration: 25 months (Full recovery by Nov 2010)

Triggered by the collapse of Lehman Brothers and the subprime mortgage crisis, this crash sent shockwaves through global markets. Yet within just over two years, the Nifty had fully recovered and moved higher.

2.) 2011 – Eurozone Debt Crisis

Fall Duration: 13 months (Nov 2010 – Dec 2011)

% Fall: -28%

Recovery Duration: 12 months (Full recovery by Dec 2012)

Concerns over European countries' debt triggered a worldwide sell-off. Patient investors saw the market rebound in just a year.

3.) 2015 – China Slowdown, Commodity Crash & 2016 Demonetisation Impact

Fall Duration: 11 months (Mar 2015 – Feb 2016)

% Fall: -23%

Recovery Duration: 14 months (Full recovery by Apr 2017)

A slowdown in China's economy and a global commodity crash weighed on markets. In India, the demonetisation announcement in November 2016 briefly added pressure, but the recovery came strong.

4.) 2020 – COVID-19 Crash

Fall Duration: 3 months (Jan 2020 – Mar 2020)

% Fall: -39%

Recovery Duration: 8 months (Full recovery by Nov 2020)

One of the fastest crashes in history was also followed by one of the fastest recoveries, proving the resilience of markets in the face of global uncertainty.

5.) 2022 – Global Inflation, Interest Rate Hikes & Russia–Ukraine War

Fall Duration: 8 months (Oct 2021 – Jun 2022)

% Fall: -18%

Recovery Duration: 15 months (Full recovery by Sep 2023)

The combination of high inflation, aggressive interest rate hikes, and the geopolitical shock of the Russia–Ukraine war created volatility, but once again, the market rebounded to new highs.

Usually, such "red years" in the stock market last for approximately three years. In your investment journey, as outlined in earlier chapters, the focus should consistently be on the long term (15+ Years). Even if two separate phases of three-year declines occur, we should view them as opportunities rather than threats. Why? Because during such downturns, the average purchase price of our mutual fund units gets lowered, allowing us to accumulate more units at cheaper prices. This strategy sets the stage for higher compounding when the market recovers.

Over the last 35 years, markets have faced countless internal and external challenges — from political instability, policy changes, and economic crises to global wars and pandemics. During COVID-19, we were uncertain about our very futures, yet the markets recovered strongly. This history teaches us one vital lesson: downturns are temporary, but the market's long-term growth potential is permanent for those who stay invested.

💡 **Remember: Falls are temporary, but growth is permanent.**

5

Mutual Funds – The Basics You Need to Know

An Easy Way to Make Your Money Work for You.

When I first heard the term "Mutual Fund," I imagined something complicated — charts, stock markets, finance jargon. It sounded like something meant only for experts or rich people.

But when I finally understood what it really meant, I smiled.

Because it was actually designed for people like us.

So… What Exactly is a Mutual Fund?

A Mutual Fund is like a financial co-operative.

Think of it this way:

• You, me, and thousands of others put money into a common pool.

- That pool is managed by professional fund managers.
- These experts use the pooled money to invest in stocks, bonds, gold, real estate, etc.
- The returns earned are shared back with all investors — based on how much they invested.

It's safe (regulated by SEBI), transparent, and accessible to everyone — even if you're starting with just ₹500/month.

Why Mutual Funds Are Brilliant for Beginners.

Here's what makes Mutual Funds the smartest starting point for most people:

1. Low Entry Barrier

One of the biggest advantages of mutual funds for beginners is that you don't need a large amount of money to start investing. With options like SIPs (Systematic Investment Plans), you can begin with as little as ₹500 a month—an amount most people can comfortably set aside. This makes it possible to start your investment journey without waiting to accumulate a big lump sum. More importantly, it allows you to develop the habit of investing regularly, which is the real key to building wealth over time.

2. Expert Management

When you invest in mutual funds, your money is managed by professional fund managers who have the knowledge, experience, and resources to make informed investment decisions. They research companies, study market trends, and diversify investments to manage risk—something most beginners would struggle to do on their own. This means you can benefit from expert-level decision-making without having to constantly track the markets yourself, making mutual funds a stress-free and efficient way to grow your wealth.

3. Diversification

When you invest in an equity mutual fund, your money is typically spread across 70–80 different companies.

This means even if 3–5 of them underperform, the impact on your overall investment is minimal because the fund manager can quickly identify the laggards and replace them with better-performing stocks. Look at the image above—many of these companies like Infosys, HDFC Bank, D-Mart, Tata, Asian Paints, Reliance, and Airtel are brands we use or interact with in our daily lives.

By investing in a single mutual fund, you indirectly own a part of these companies, enjoying the benefits of their growth without having to individually buy and monitor each stock.

This is the true power of diversification—it keeps your portfolio resilient while keeping your investing simple.

4. Flexibility

Mutual funds offer a level of flexibility that's hard to match. You can start or stop your investments whenever you want, increase or decrease the amount based on your financial situation, or redeem your money partially or fully without complicated processes (except in certain lock-in schemes like ELSS). Whether you want to invest monthly through SIPs, make lump-sum contributions, or switch between funds as your goals change, mutual funds adapt to your needs. This flexibility ensures that your investments grow alongside your life's changing priorities and circumstances.

5. Liquidity

One of the biggest advantages of mutual funds is liquidity—the ease with which you can access your money. Unlike fixed deposits or other locked-in investments, most mutual funds allow you to redeem your units at any time and have the money credited to your bank account within a couple of working days. This is a huge contrast to real estate, where selling can take weeks, months, or even years, involves heavy transaction costs, and—most importantly—you can't sell just half your property if you only need part of the money. With mutual funds, you can redeem exactly the amount you require, making them far more flexible and convenient in meeting your financial needs.

6. Transparency & Regulation

As to be discussed later in the book, one of the key strengths of mutual funds is the high level of transparency and strict regulation they operate under. In India, mutual funds are regulated by SEBI (Securities and Exchange Board of India), which ensures that fund houses follow clear guidelines, disclose all portfolio details, and maintain ethical practices. You can easily track where your money is invested, how the fund is performing, and what costs you are paying—information that is updated regularly and publicly available. This level of openness, combined with strong regulatory oversight, gives investors' confidence and peace of mind that their money is being managed responsibly.

Types of Mutual Funds:

There are hundreds of funds, but here's the simplest way to understand them:

□ **Equity Funds (High Return, High Growth, Long-Term)**

- Invest mostly in company shares.
- Ideal for wealth creation over 7–10+ years.

□ **Debt Funds (Stable, Low Risk, Short-Term)**

- Invest in government bonds, corporate debt.
- Ideal for 1–3 years or conservative goals.

□ **Hybrid Funds (Balanced Approach)**

- Mix of equity + debt.
- Suitable for medium-term, balanced investors.

Think of it like a thali:

- Equity is the spicy curry (growth).
- Debt is the plain rice (stability).
- Hybrid is the balanced meal.

Real-Life Example:

Let me introduce you to Sneha, a spirited young client of mine — a 29-year-old entrepreneur who owns and runs a thriving beauty parlour exclusively for women. Through her dedication and skill, she has built a loyal customer base, and after covering all her business expenses, she takes home an average monthly income of ₹45,000. Instead of keeping all her savings in her bank account, she started a Systematic Investment Plan (SIP) of ₹8,000/month in a good equity mutual fund.

Over the next 20 years, assuming 12% annual returns, her investment grows to ₹73.5 lakhs (₹19.2 lakhs invested)

From just ₹8,000/month!

No extra work. No trading. Just patience and discipline.

Now imagine Sneha takes it one step further. Every year, she increases her SIP by just ₹800/month (thanks to her growing business). That small step-up turns her final wealth into a massive ₹1.17 crore (₹37.44 lakhs invested) — without feeling a big pinch in her monthly budget. You know the best part? If she continues it for additional 5 years, the corpus doubles in just the next 5 years! Her corpus would now grow to a whopping ₹2.28 Crores (₹52.8 lakhs invested).

Let that sink in!

So, Who Should Invest in Mutual Funds?

- A 24-year-old starting their career.
- A 35-year-old planning for kids' education/higher education.
- A 45-year-old building retirement income.
- New parents - in the name of their newly born child.
- A retail shop owner.
- An entrepreneur.
- Even senior citizens looking for better income options than FDs.

If you have a financial goal — there's a mutual fund for you.

One More Thing: It's NOT Just About Returns.

Mutual funds offer more than high returns.

They offer:

- **Peace of mind**
- **Time freedom**
- **A system that grows quietly while you live your life**

In the next chapter, we'll answer the big question everyone asks:

"But are Mutual Funds safe?"

6

Are Mutual Funds Safe?

Let's Bust the Biggest Myth

Whenever I talk to someone new about mutual funds, the first question is usually:

"Is it safe?"

The second?

"What if I lose all my money?"

I get it. Fear is natural — especially when it comes to money.

We have all seen TV ads run by Association of Mutual Funds in India (AMFI) while the IPL cricket matches are on. Why does the ad say "Mutual Fund investments are subject to market risks"? if at all this book is claiming that Mutual Funds are actually really safe?

Here's the truth:

Mutual Funds are one of the most regulated, transparent, and professionally managed financial tools in India.

Let's break this down.

How Mutual Funds Are Structured in India:

Every Mutual Fund company — or as we call it, an Asset Management Company (AMC) — in India is:

- Registered with SEBI (Securities and Exchange Board of India)
- Operated under the Indian Trusts Act, 1882
- Bound by the SEBI Mutual Fund Regulations, 1996
- Mutual Fund Distributors (MFD), who guide you through your investment journey, are registered with the Association of Mutual Funds in India (AMFI) and are bound by the code of conduct prescribed by AMFI.

It's not some random "scheme." It's a legal trust, governed by professionals and monitored tightly.

In fact, even your SIP money doesn't go to the AMC (Asset Management Company) directly.

It goes to the custodian bank, held separately and securely.

No mutual fund company can just run away with your money, nor any Mutual Fund Distributor (MFD) who guides you.

But Markets Go Up and Down, and so do all the asset classes..."

Yes. And that's exactly why you don't invest blindly and hence the disclaimer, "Mutual Fund investments are subject to market risks". You invest based on your goal and time horizon with the help of a good Mutual Fund Distributor (MFD).

Let's take an example on how economic condition impacts not just equity markets but also gold and real estate. Suppose you buy a house worth ₹50 lakhs today. Two years later, the economy faces a slowdown as severe as the 2008 crisis. In that period, let's say no one is even offering you ₹40 lakhs for the property you bought at ₹50 lakhs.

What would you do? Would you panic and sell it off at a random price say ₹40 lakhs? Or ₹35 lakhs? just because the buyer is available at that price? Or would you hold on, knowing the basics of the real estate market — that prices recover over time — and wait for the right moment to gain appreciation before selling, if at all you wish to sell?

The same applies to gold. Between 2011 and 2019, gold prices dropped by nearly 30% from their peak. Did any of you rush to sell your gold during those years? Probably not. You held on because you knew its value would recover eventually.

So why panic when mutual funds drop for a year or two? In fact, if you're investing via SIP, market slowdowns and "red days" are actually a boon — because you accumulate more units at lower prices.

This instant visibility of mutual fund values on an app in your phone, while a huge advantage, can also play tricks on your emotions. Because you can see your portfolio's worth changing every single day—sometimes even dropping sharply when markets fall—it's easy to panic and feel the urge to sell. That constant flow of numbers can make short-term losses feel bigger and more urgent than they really are.

With real estate or gold, you don't face this emotional rollercoaster as intensely. Since you can't track their value on an app every day, you're less likely to react to every small fluctuation. The news of the prices coming down probably doesn't even reach you. You might only check property prices once in a few years or gold rates occasionally, so temporary dips often pass unnoticed. In a way, the lack of instant updates acts as an emotional buffer, while mutual funds require you to train your mind to focus on the long-term goal rather than the daily noise.

In fact, no one even thinks of selling gold or real estate in their entire life— so why would you even consider selling mutual funds in a loss, especially when mutual funds have the potential to yield a higher CAGR (Compound Annual Growth Rate) than both gold and real estate? So, to still be on a safer side, we follow the below mentioned golden rule.

Here's the golden rule:

Short-term money ≠ Equity Funds

Long-term money = Equity Funds

Ultra-short term money = Debt or Liquid Funds

Example:

- If you need money in 6 months → Use Liquid Funds
- If you want to build wealth over 10 years → Use Equity Mutual Funds SIPs

Most people lose money in mutual funds because they panic when markets fall.

But what they forget is — **the fall is temporary, growth is permanent** — as discussed just now and dissected in the earlier chapters.

Some Reassuring Facts

As of today, the total amount of money invested in mutual funds in India—measured by Assets Under Management (AUM)—stands at approximately ₹75.36 lakh crore (₹75.36 trillion) - July 31, 2025 (Source - AMFI India)

Here's how that number has evolved across recent months:

March 2025 saw AUM cross the ₹70 lakh crore milestone.

June 2025, AUM was about ₹74.40 lakh crore

July 2025 brought a new high, reaching ₹75.36 lakh crore, according to AMFI.

So yes, as of July 2025, mutual funds in India collectively manage over ₹75 lakh crore—making mutual funds one of the biggest investment platforms in the country — yet many of us hesitate to even start a simple SIP of ₹10,000.

- Lakhs of government employees, NRIs, retirees, and even companies use mutual funds.

- You receive account statements, NAV reports, and real-time tracking via apps and email.

- No lock-in period in most funds (except ELSS — which has a 3-year lock-in).

You're always in control.

You know what **The Real Risk** is? It's **Not Investing**.

Let me ask you:

• Is your FD keeping up with inflation?

• Do you have a plan to make your money work harder than you do?

• Are you even investing enough?

If the answer is no — then "not investing" is riskier than "investing".

“Wealth is not created by avoiding risk. It’s created by managing risk smartly.”

Mutual Funds help you do exactly that.

In the next chapter, we’ll meet your new wealth-building partner:

The Systematic Investment Plan (SIP) — and why it could change your life.

7

SIP – Your Monthly Wealth Machine

The Best Investment Habit You'll Ever Build.

If Mutual Funds are the vehicle to wealth, then SIP is the fuel.

And it's not just any fuel — it's automated, consistent, and unbelievably powerful.

Let me take you back to when I met Shivakaran, a 27-year-old schoolteacher. He told me:

"I don't have lakhs to invest. I can barely save ₹2,000/month. Should I even bother?"

My answer?

YES. And that ₹2,000 could make you a **millionaire**.

What is SIP?

SIP stands for Systematic Investment Plan.

It's a simple way to invest a fixed amount every month into a mutual fund — just like an EMI, but in reverse.

Instead of paying interest, you're now earning wealth.

SIP does 3 beautiful things:

1. Builds Discipline – Money gets auto-debited.

2. Manages Risk – You invest at different market levels (rupee cost averaging).

3. Creates Habit – Small amounts become big wealth over time.

How SIP Transforms Your Future:

Let's say you invest just ₹5,000/month through SIP at an average return of 12%.

Years	Total Invested	Corpus Value
5	₹ 3,00,000	₹ 4,05,000
10	₹ 6,00,000	₹ 11,20,000
15	₹ 9,00,000	₹ 23,80,000
20	₹ 12,00,000	₹ 46,00,000
25	₹ 15,00,000	₹ 85,11,000
30	₹ 18,00,000	₹ 1,54,00,000

Ideal case scenario of a ₹5,000/Month SIP @ 12 CAGR

This table beautifully shows the **power of compounding** in Mutual Fund SIP investments. By investing just ₹5,000 per month, the invested amount grows steadily over the years. In 5 years, an investment of ₹3 lakh grows to ₹4.05 lakh, but when continued for 20 years, ₹12 lakh becomes ₹46 lakhs. The real magic happens in the long run — in 30 years, a total investment of ₹18 lakh grows into an impressive ₹1.54 crore. This clearly proves that **time in the market is more important than timing the market**, and disciplined investing can help create substantial wealth.

Now increase your SIP by just ₹500 every year, and corpus reaches to ₹2.66 Crores with an investment of just ₹44.10 lakhs over the 30 years' duration as shown in the below chart!

Years	Total Invested	Corpus Value
5	₹ 3,60,000	₹ 4,77,400
10	₹ 8,70,000	₹ 15,21,700
15	₹ 15,30,000	₹ 35,64,800
20	₹ 23,40,000	₹ 73,68,100
25	₹ 33,00,000	₹ 1,42,73,700
30	₹ 44,10,000	₹ 2,66,46,400

Ideal case scenario of a ₹5,000/Month with ₹500/Month Annual Step Up SIP @ 12 CAGR

Why Step Up? Because your salary and income keep growing with time, and adding just ₹500 extra per month every year hardly pinches the pocket — but it creates a huge difference in your long-term wealth.

SIP rewards consistency, not cleverness.

You don't need to time the market — you just need to spend time in the market.

You won't see results in the first few months or even years. Compounding doesn't even kick in until 7 years! Sometimes markets will dip.

You may feel like stopping.

But SIP teaches you a life-changing lesson:

Good habits are boring, but they make you rich.

In any field, it's often the boring, repetitive work that quietly builds real wealth. Just like a farmer patiently sowing seeds and tending to his crops season after season, sticking to the "boring" process pays off big in the long run.

You may not notice change in year 3 or 5.

But by year 7 or 10 — when your corpus starts growing faster than your income — you'll understand why SIP is magic.

Real-Life Example

Let's take the example of Aakash, who recently moved his investments from his previous Mutual Fund Distributor as he wasn't satisfied with his service and transferred his portfolio under my ARN (AMFI Registration Number allotted to all Mutual Fund Distributors by AMFI).

He started a ₹2,000 SIP at age 27.

He increased it by ₹500 every year.

Today, at 42, he has over ₹30+ lakhs in his portfolio.

No side hustle. No trading. Just simple, boring SIPs.

And the best part?

he doesn't even "feel" the investment anymore.

It became a habit — like a mobile bill. Only this bill pays him back.

How to Start Your SIP?

1. Choose your goal (retirement, education, house, etc.)
2. Select a mutual fund category (Equity/Hybrid/Debt)
3. Start with any platform or registered distributor
4. Set your SIP amount — even ₹500 is fine!
5. Link your bank account — and you're done!

Sit back. Let it run.

Check once a year. Don't panic in between.

"SIP is like planting a tree. Water it monthly. Wait patiently. One day, it will give shade, fruits, and security."

The 3 Golden SIP Rules:

1. Start Early – Time is your biggest ally.
2. Stay Consistent – Don't stop during market falls.
3. Step-Up – Increase your SIP with income growth.

In the next chapter, I'll show you what happens when people delay this powerful habit… and how even a few years can cost you crores.

8

The Cost of Delay

A Lesson That Can Save You Crores

Let me tell you about two friends — Ramesh and Suresh.

They both started working at age 25. Both earned similar salaries. Both wanted to invest. But here's what happened:

- Ramesh started an SIP of ₹5,000/month at age 25.
- Suresh delayed. He started the same SIP at age 30 — just 5 years later.

Both continued their SIP till they turned 55 (25 years for Suresh, 30 years for Ramesh). Now let's see the result — assuming 12% returns:

Investor	Total Invested	Final Corpus at 55
Ramesh	₹ 18,00,000	₹ 1.54 Crores
Suresh	₹ 15,00,000	₹ 85 Lakhs

Ramesh ends up with ₹69 lakhs more with an extra investment of just ₹3,00,000 — just because he started 5 years earlier. That's the benefit of starting yearly! And that's the cost of delay for those who keep doubting Mutual Funds!

"But I'll Start When I Earn More..." I hear this a lot.

People in their 20s or 30s say, "Let me wait till I earn better. I'll start investing later." The truth? If you can spend on Netflix, coffee, gadgets, and random things each month — you can invest too. Even a small SIP of ₹1,000/month started early is better than ₹10,000/month started late.

Adding one more self-explanatory table below to make you understand how important it is to start early with whatever amount feels comfortable to you. You can always increase it later on.

			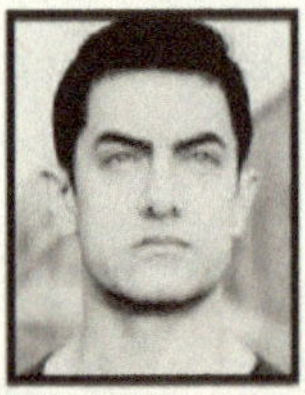
AMOUNT INVESTED	15,000 PER MONTH	15,000 PER MONTH	15,000 PER MONTH
STARTING AGE	25 YEAR OLD	35 YEAR OLD	45 YEAR OLD
RETURN PER ANNUM (%)	12%	12%	12%
RETIRE @ AGE	65	65	65
EXPECTED AMOUNT	14.70 CRORE	4.62 CRORE	1.38 CRORE
START INVESTING EARLY			

The table below clearly shows how, every five years, the amount you need to invest to reach your goal, doubles. This illustrates how even the smallest investments, when planned well within time, can help you achieve your target with ease.

SIP Amount Needed To Reach ₹ 2 Crore @ 60 Years Age	
AGE	**SIP Amount Needed**
25	₹ 1,800/-
30	₹ 3,600/-
35	₹ 7,300/-
40	₹ 15,100/-
45	₹ 33,000/-
Assuming 15% CAGR	

SIP Requirement Doubling After Every 5 Years Delay

Compounding Has One Rule: Respect Time

Compounding doesn't reward:

- Intelligence
- Income
- Luck

It only rewards time + consistency.

Every year you delay is not just a lost year of investment — it's a lost decade of compounding.

Imagine skipping 1 year of SIP at ₹5,000.

At 12% return over 30 years, that skipped ₹60,000 would have grown to ₹17.5 lakhs.

A Simple Exercise:

Ask yourself:

- How many years have I already delayed?
- What if I had started 5 years ago?
- What if I start today?

Don't let guilt stop you. Let it fuel action.

Because the best time to start was yesterday.

The next best time is NOW.

It's Not About Regret — It's About Restart

Whether you're 22 or 52, remember this:

"You don't need to be early. You just need to be consistent from now on."

Don't wait for the perfect time.

Don't wait for extra money.

Start with what you have — and upgrade later.

In the next chapter, I'll show you how to use your mutual fund investments not just to grow wealth — but to generate monthly income. Yes, you can literally pay your bills without even having to work for that money. Also, without ever touching your corpus.

Let's meet the Systematic Withdrawal Plan.

9

Financial Planning with SWP – Creating Monthly Income from Wealth

Retire Without Worry. Live Without Fear.

First, let's do a simple exercise to understand the concept of "Financial Planning," and by the end of this chapter, we'll dive into SWP and its importance.

Look at the chart mentioned on the next page as how our current monthly expenses keep growing with time due to inflation.

Current Monthly Expense	Monthly Expense after 10 Years	Monthly Expense after 15 Years	Monthly Expense after 20 Years	Monthly Expense after 25 Years	Monthly Expense after 30 Years
₹ 25,000	₹ 44,800	₹ 60,000	₹ 80,200	₹ 1,07,500	₹ 1,43,600
₹ 50,000	₹ 89,500	₹ 1,20,000	₹ 1,60,400	₹ 2,14,600	₹ 2,87,200
₹ 75,000	₹ 1,35,000	₹ 1,80,000	₹ 2,41,000	₹ 3,22,000	₹ 4,31,000
₹ 1,00,000	₹ 1,80,000	₹ 2,40,000	₹ 3,20,000	₹ 4,30,000	₹ 5,75,000
₹ 1,50,000	₹ 2,70,000	₹ 3,60,000	₹ 4,82,000	₹ 6,44,000	₹ 8,62,000
₹ 2,00,000	₹ 3,60,000	₹ 4,80,000	₹ 6,42,000	₹ 8,60,000	₹ 11,50,000

Current Household Expenses V/s 6 % Inflation and Time

Looking at the chart, it's clear how inflation quietly but powerfully makes you spend more over time. Let's take an example: if your current monthly expenses are ₹50,000, with inflation assumed at 6% per year, in 25 years the same lifestyle will cost you around ₹2 lakhs per month. That's over four times your current spending — without any change in your living standard. This means that the ₹50,000 you manage comfortably with today will feel like barely enough in the future, unless your income or investments grow at least in line with inflation. That's why disciplined investing and regularly increasing your savings, is crucial. Simply saving a fixed amount in a bank account won't work — your money must grow faster than inflation if you want to maintain, or improve, your lifestyle over the long term.

Let's continue with the same example and assume your current monthly expense is ₹50,000. In 25 years, you would need about ₹2,00,000 per month to maintain the same standard of living. Sounds crazy, right? Don't worry — I've got you. That's exactly why we're doing this exercise.

Now, I'll show you a plan to get this ₹2 Lakh per month credited to your bank account as a salary for a lifetime — without having to work for it!

Monthly Income Needed	Total Corpus Needed
₹ 1,00,000	2 Cr
₹ 1,50,000	3 Cr
₹ 2,00,000	4 Cr
₹ 2,50,000	5 Cr
₹ 3,00,000	6 Cr
₹ 4,00,000	8 Cr

Monthly Income Needed to Corpus Needed Ratio

So, as per the chart, we need to have a corpus of ₹4 crores ready in the next 25 years to generate a monthly income of ₹2,00,000 thereafter. How do we achieve that? Doesn't it seem like a hefty amount to accumulate? Will simply saving a small amount every month help? Let's find out by studying the below chart.

In the below chart, **savings** is taken in the literal sense — meaning you are simply putting money aside without investing it. This does not refer to keeping money in a bank's savings account, where at least a 2%–3% annual interest is earned. But even that small return is not enough to beat inflation. True wealth creation happens only when money is allowed to work for you through disciplined investing, not when it is left idle and losing value over time.

Savings Per Month	Savings Increase Every Year	Savings in 10 Years	Savings in 15 Years	Savings in 20 Years	Savings in 25 Years
₹ 3,000	10 %	5.73 Lakhs	11.44 Lakhs	20.62 Lakhs	35.40 Lakhs
₹ 5,000	10 %	9.56 Lakhs	19.06 Lakhs	34.36 Lakhs	59.00 Lakhs
₹ 8,000	10 %	15.30 Lakhs	30.50 Lakhs	54.99 Lakhs	94.41 Lakhs
₹ 10,000	10 %	19.12 Lakhs	38.12 Lakhs	68.73 Lakhs	1.18 Crore
₹ 15,000	10 %	28.69 Lakhs	57.19 Lakhs	1.03 Crore	1.77 Crore
₹ 20,000	10 %	38.24 Lakhs	76.25 Lakhs	1.37 Crore	2.36 Crore
₹ 25,000	10 %	47.81 Lakhs	95.31 Lakhs	1.71 Crore	2.95 Crore

Incremental Savings Over a Period of 25 Years

Ah! Saving ₹20,000 per month while increasing savings by 10% every year still gets us to a just ₹1.37 Crore in 20 years while we are targeting ₹4 crores, and we barely reach ₹2.36 Crore in 25 years — falling behind by a whopping ₹1.64 crores of our actual ₹4 crore target. And this is after increasing your savings by 10% annually — without even being sure if your salary will actually grow at that rate in the long run! Now what? How do we reach a ₹4 crore corpus without having to save ₹20,000 every month? Is there still a way? Definitely YES! Keep calm and follow along!

Spend about 10 minutes on the chart below to understand how SIP can get you to ₹4 crores without having to save ₹20,000 per month. Also, notice what happens when you continue the SIP for another 5 years, and then another 5 years after that. You'll get a clear picture of how SIP works and how much SIP is needed to cover your monthly expenses after 25 years — without having to work for that money.

SIP / Month	Yearly Step Up SIP	Invested Amount Vs Return After 10 Years	Invested Amount Vs Return After 15 Years
₹ 5,000	₹ 500	8.70 Lakhs | 17.60 Lakhs	15.30 Lakhs | 44.88 Lakhs
₹ 7,000	₹ 700	12.18 Lakhs | 24.64 Lakhs	21.42 Lakhs | 62.84 Lakhs
₹ 10,000	₹ 1,000	17.40 Lakhs | 35.20 Lakhs	30.60 Lakhs | 89.77 Lakhs
₹ 12,000	₹ 1,200	20.88 Lakhs | 42.24 Lakhs	36.72 Lakhs | 1.07 Cr
₹ 15,000	₹1,500	26.10 Lakhs | 52.80 Lakh	45.90 Lakhs | 1.34 Cr
₹ 25,000	₹ 2,500	43.50 Lakh | 88 Lakhs	76.50 Lakhs | 2.24 Cr
₹ 50,000	₹ 5,000	87 Lakhs | 1.76 Cr	1.53 Cr | 4.48 Cr
₹ 75,000	₹ 7,500	1.31 Cr | 2.64 Cr	2.30 Cr | 6.73 Cr
₹ 1,00,000	₹ 10,000	1.74 Cr | 3.52 Cr	3.06 Cr | 8.97 Cr

SIP Table: Assumed CAGR-15%

SIP / Month	Yearly Step Up SIP	Invested Amount Vs Return After 20 Years	Invested Amount Vs Return After 25 Years
₹ 5,000	₹ 500	23.40 Lakhs | 1.01 Cr	33 Lakhs | 2.18 Cr
₹ 7,000	₹ 700	32.76 Lakhs | 1.42 Cr	46.20 Lakhs | 3.06 Cr
₹ 10,000	₹ 1,000	46.80 Lakhs | 2.03 Cr	66 Lakhs | 4.37 Cr
₹ 12,000	₹ 1,200	56.16 Lakhs | 2.44 Cr	79.20 Lakhs | 5.25 Cr
₹ 15,000	₹1,500	70.20 Lakhs | 3.05 Cr	99 Lakhs | 6.56 Cr
₹ 25,000	₹ 2,500	1.17 Cr | 5.09 Cr	1.65 Cr | 10.94 Cr
₹ 50,000	₹ 5,000	2.34 Cr | 10.19 Cr	3.3 Cr | 21.89 Cr
₹ 75,000	₹ 7,500	3.51 Cr | 15.29 Cr	4.95 Cr | 32.83 Cr
₹ 1,00,000	₹ 10,000	4.68 Cr | 20.39 Cr	6.60 Cr | 43.78 Cr

SIP Table: Assumed CAGR-15%

SIP / Month	Yearly Step Up SIP	Invested Amount Vs Return After 30 Years	Invested Amount Vs Return After 35 Years
₹ 5,000	₹ 500	44.10 Lakhs | 4.56 Cr	56.70 Lakhs | 9.36 Cr
₹ 7,000	₹ 700	61.75 Lakhs | 6.39 Cr	79.38 Lakhs | 13.10 Cr
₹ 10,000	₹ 1,000	88.20 Lakhs | 9.12 Cr	88.20 Lakhs | 9.12 Cr
₹ 12,000	₹ 1,200	1.05 Cr | 11 Cr	1.13 Cr | 18.70 Cr
₹ 15,000	₹1,500	1.32 Cr | 13.70 Cr	1.70 Cr | 28.08 Cr
₹ 25,000	₹ 2,500	2.2 Cr | 22.90 Cr	2.83 Cr | 46.80 Cr
₹ 50,000	₹ 5,000	4.41 Cr | 45.64 Cr	5.67 Cr | 93.61 Cr
₹ 75,000	₹ 7,500	6.61 Cr | 68.40 Cr	8.50 Cr | 140.40 Cr
₹ 1,00,000	₹ 10,000	8.82 Cr | 91.3 Cr	11.34 Cr | 187.22 Cr

SIP Table: Assumed CAGR-15%

So, as per the chart, we would now need to save — or rather, invest — just ₹10,000 per month with an annual step-up of ₹1,000 per month to reach around ₹4 crores in 25 years. Mind you, saving an additional 10% annually is different from stepping up your SIP by ₹1,000 per month every year.

Difference explained:

Annual Step-Up by ₹1,000 per Month:

This means that every year, you increase your SIP amount by a fixed ₹1,000.

Example: Year 1 = ₹10,000/month, Year 2 = ₹11,000/month, Year 3 = ₹12,000/month, and so on.

This is a fixed absolute increase each year.

Annual Savings Increase by 10%:

Here, your Savings amount increases by percentage, not a fixed number.

Example: Year 1 = ₹10,000/month, Year 2 = ₹11,000/month (10% more), Year 3 = ₹12,100/month (10% more than ₹11,000), and so on.

This is a compounding increase — the increment amount grows each year.

In short:

₹1,000 step-up → fixed increase every year.

10% increase → growing (compounding) increase every year.

Now let's understand SWP in detail and its magic!

Imagine this:

You wake up on a Monday morning.

No alarm. No boss. No commute.

You sip tea, check your phone, and see a message:

"₹2,00,000 credited to your account – SWP pay-out"

And the best part? Your original investment is still growing quietly.

This isn't a dream.

This is called a Systematic Withdrawal Plan (SWP) — and it's one of the smartest ways to retire rich and live stress-free.

What is SWP? SWP stands for Systematic Withdrawal Plan. It's the opposite of SIP.

- In SIP, you invest every month.
- In SWP, you withdraw a fixed amount every month — from your mutual fund investment.

It's like giving yourself a monthly salary from your own wealth — while your money continues to stay invested and grow.

The Ideal Retirement Plan

Let's take the earlier example and say you've built a mutual fund corpus of ₹4.37 Crore at the age of 55 by starting an SIP of ₹10,000/month and ₹1,000 annual step-up @ 15% CAGR 25 years ago as we have studied through the charts mentioned earlier.

Now instead of withdrawing the entire ₹4.37 Crore amount or putting it into a fixed deposit (which gives poor returns), you set up an SWP of ₹2,00,000/month (Yearly 6% of your corpus). Now let's study the below image and experience the power of SWP.

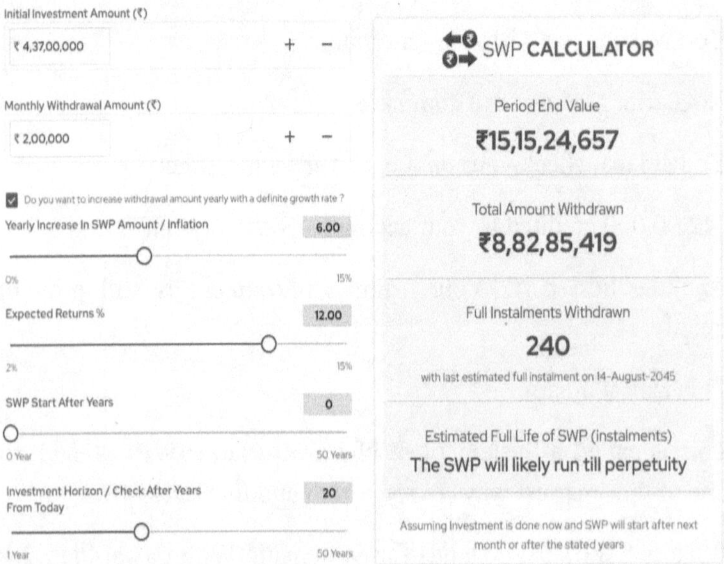

As stated earlier you start receiving ₹2,00,000 every month out of your corpus of ₹4.37 crore, just like a salary, but without having to work for it. Even better, this monthly income will grow by additional 6% apart from 6% withdrawal every year to match inflation, ensuring your purchasing power remains intact. Over 20 years, you would have withdrawn a massive ₹8.82 crore in total, and yet, your investment would still be worth ₹15.15 crore at the end of the 20-year period. This is the true magic of an SWP (Systematic Withdrawal Plan) — your money keeps paying you for decades while simultaneously growing in value, creating the perfect balance of income and wealth preservation, almost like having a money-making machine that never stops.

This is financial freedom.

This is how one builds generational wealth.

The reason SWP works is simple math. Your corpus grows at an annual rate of around 12% CAGR in hybrid funds, while you withdraw only 6% per year — split into 0.5% monthly instalments. Even if your investments were to return just 10% annually, you would still be left with nearly ₹7.4 crore at the end of 20 years' period. It's really as simple as that!

Real-Life Example

Let me tell you about Mr. and Mrs. Jadhav— retired school principal in Solapur.

They had a combined corpus of ₹70 lakhs.

We helped them set up an SWP of ₹35,000/month from a mix of hybrid and equity mutual funds.

5 years later:

- They're still receiving regular income.
- Their original ₹70 lakhs have grown to ₹94 lakhs despite withdrawals.
- No rent, no pension worry, no tension.

"We sleep peacefully," Mrs. Jadhav once told me. "It's like our investments are working for us now."

How is This Better Than Rental Yield from Property/Flat?

Many people rely on rent from flats or houses post-retirement. But let's compare:

Type	Flat	SWP
Investment	50 Lakhs	50 Lakhs
Property Tax	Applicable	Not Applicable
Broker Charges	Applicable	Not Applicable
Renovation Charges	Applicable	Not Applicable
Rental Loss	Applicable	Not Applicable
Average Returns	10k - 12k / Month	25k / Month
Capital Appreciation	8% - 9%	12 %

Rental Yield: Flat V/s SWP in Mutual Funds

The comparison clearly highlights the differences between investing ₹50 lakhs in a flat versus a Systematic Withdrawal Plan (SWP). While a flat involves ongoing expenses like property tax, broker fees, renovation charges, and potential rental losses, an SWP eliminates all these costs. In terms of returns, a ₹50 lakh worth flat typically generates ₹10k–₹12k per month in India, whereas an SWP can provide ₹25k per month. Even in capital appreciation, SWP stands ahead with an average of 10% - 12% compared to 8% - 9% for property. Additionally, SWPs are generally more tax-efficient, as they are subject to capital gains tax—which can be lower and more flexible—rather than the multiple taxes and charges associated with real estate ownership. This makes SWP a more profitable and hassle-free investment choice in the long run.

SWP offers flexibility, better returns, and peace of mind — especially for retirees.

Fixed Deposits V/s SWP

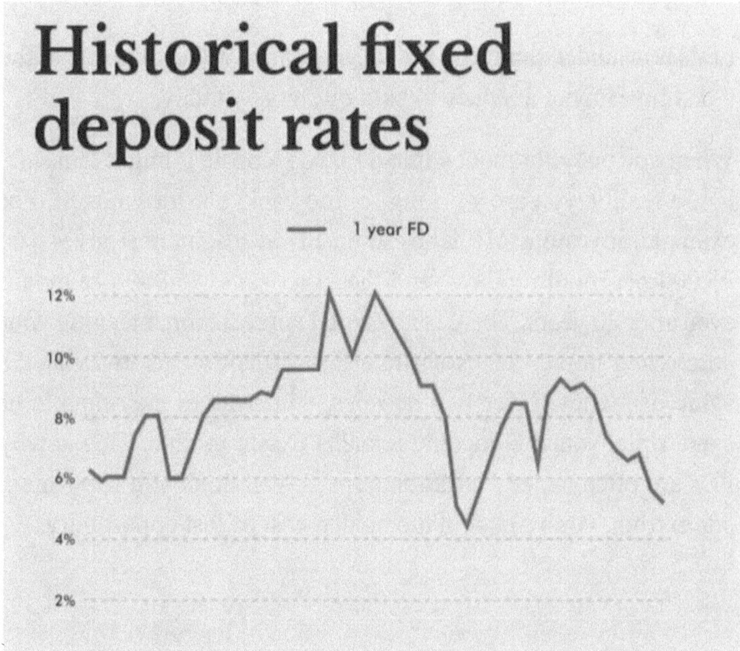

As indicated in the chart on the previous page, the historical trend of Fixed Deposit (FD) rates in India, reveals a clear long-term decline. In the early 1990s, 1-year FD rates peaked at over 12%, offering highly attractive returns for conservative investors. However, since then, rates have steadily reduced, with occasional spikes, and now hover near 6%—among the lowest in decades. This fall is not unique to India; it mirrors the pattern seen in developed nations like the USA, where fixed deposit rates are often much lower, typically between 0.5%–3% per annum in recent years. As an economy matures, inflation tends to stabilize, the cost of capital decreases, and interest rates naturally decline. For India, this means that as we progress towards becoming a fully developed economy, FD rates are likely to keep trending downward. This shift underscores the importance of exploring alternative investment avenues, such as equities and mutual funds, to outpace inflation and grow wealth effectively.

Let's now understand why Fixed Deposits have become one of the worst investment avenues to park our money today.

When you put your money into a Fixed Deposit, it might feel safe, but in reality, you are working for the bank, not for yourself. For example, investing ₹10 lakhs in an FD at 6% interest gives you ₹5,000 per month today—and the exact same ₹5,000 per month even after 20 years. There is no capital appreciation, meaning your purchasing power keeps shrinking as inflation eats away at the value of money. Over two decades, while prices may double or even triple, your FD income remains frozen in time. This is why FDs are often called "inflation traps"—you think you're earning, but in truth, you're paying the hidden cost of lost opportunity.

Amount Invested In FD	10 Lakhs
Interest Gained Per Year	6%
Per Month Income	5,000/-
Capital Appreciation	0
Base Capital After 20 Years	10 Lakhs
Per Month Income After 20 Years	5,000/-

Amount Invested In SWP	10 Lakhs
Interest Gained Per Year	6%
Per Month Income	5,000/-
Capital Appreciation	12% in Long Term
Base Capital After 20 Years	51.38 Lakhs
Per Month Income After 20 Years	25,000/-

On the other hand, a Systematic Withdrawal Plan (SWP) in mutual funds also starts by giving you ₹5,000 per month, but here's the difference—this money gets credited to your bank account every month like a salary, without having to wait for the investment tenure to end like as in FD. At the same time, your invested capital grows with market returns, and in the long term (at 12% average returns), your ₹10 lakhs could grow to over ₹51 lakhs in 20 years, giving you ₹25,000 per month then—five times the FD income—while beating inflation and building wealth. Choosing an FD over SWP is like locking your money in a box that loses value, while SWP keeps your cash flow alive and your capital growing. Although, one thing to keep in mind is that in the first 2–3 years, your invested ₹10 lakhs might show a lower value — say ₹9.3 lakh or even ₹8.7 lakh — depending on market conditions. On the other hand, it could also grow to ₹11.3 lakh or ₹12.1 lakh if the markets move favourably. Over time, however, the power of compounding combined with the market's natural tendency to grow will likely take your ₹10 lakh closer to ₹20 lakhs in 10 years, as seen in the historical data of many funds. The key point is that this short-term volatility in your invested capital will not affect the SWP amount you've chosen to withdraw. Let that be crystal clear.

How to Set Up an SWP

1. Build a corpus through SIPs or Lumpsum over time.

2. Choose a Hybrid with long-term track record.

3. Start an SWP — choose monthly amount and date. (usually we recommend not more than 0.5% monthly withdrawal of the invested corpus)

4. Monitor once a year with your advisor.

Note: You can always pause, increase, or stop your SWP as per your needs.

The Emotional Benefit of SWP

You've worked hard all your life.

Don't let your retirement be filled with fear or dependency.

SWP gives you the confidence to say: "I don't need to ask anyone for money — not my kids, not my boss, not the government."

It's not just money. It's dignity.

EMI Vs SIP

The image on the next page give us an eye-opening comparison between EMI (Equated Monthly Instalment) and SIP (Systematic Investment Plan). A home loan of ₹50,00,000 at 9% interest for 25 years demands a monthly EMI of ₹41,960. Over the tenure, the borrower shells out ₹1,25,87,945, of which ₹75,87,945 is just interest! That means the bank doesn't just lend you money, it literally owns your house until the last EMI is paid — you pay nearly 2.5 times the actual cost of your dream home.

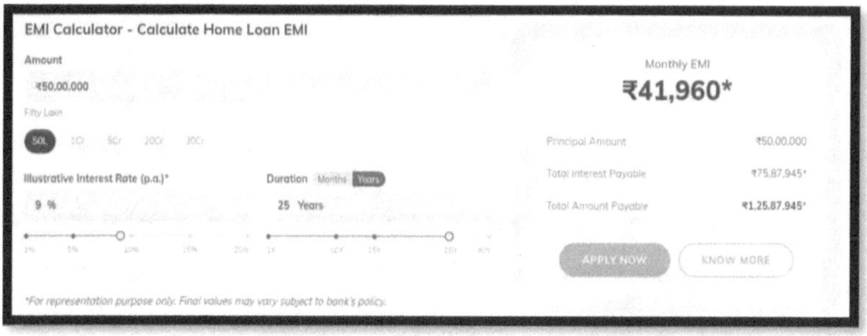

Now imagine an alternative: instead of rushing into a loan, your pre-plan 12 years in advance. If you start a SIP of ₹42,000 — the same as the EMI — and earn a 15% annual return, you would accumulate around ₹1.57 crore in just 12 years. That's enough to buy your dream home in hard cash, without pledging your next 25 years to the bank. No EMI pressure, no interest burden — you get financial freedom with ownership from day one. This option is ideal for those who haven't yet taken a home loan but want to avoid the trap of becoming a tenant to the bank.

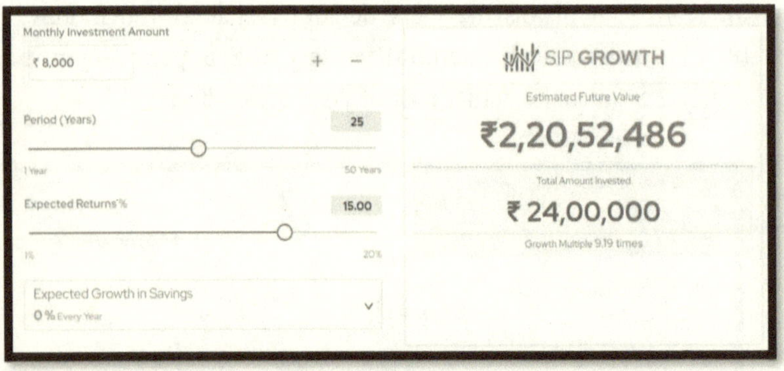

For those already paying EMI, freedom is still possible. Instead of trying to prepay the loan aggressively, simply start a SIP worth 20% of your EMI (around ₹8,000 in this example). Over the same 25 years, this grows into a massive ₹2.20 crore, while your house loan gets paid off as scheduled. In other words, at the end of 25 years you have both — a fully paid-off home and nearly ₹2 crores in cash. Even if you decide to prepay your loan in 15 years, you can continue the SIP with the reduced EMI amount, ensuring wealth creation continues till the original tenure ends. This strategy turns your EMI journey from a burden into a parallel wealth-building engine.

Insurance

You know what is more important than all of the topics we've covered in this entire book? It's health insurance and term insurance. When it comes to protecting your family's financial future, these two tools serve very different purposes and a very important one at that. Health insurance is a must for every family member, as it safeguards your savings from being wiped out by medical expenses. Term insurance, on the other hand, should be taken only for the person who is earning and financially supporting the family. The purpose of term insurance is to replace the breadwinner's income in case of an untimely death, ensuring that dependents can continue their lives without financial distress. This coverage should ideally last only until the earning member is expected to work or until the next generation begins earning and becomes financially independent. After that stage, the need for term insurance naturally fades, as the family's financial dependency has already reduced or ended.

One more topic I want to cover before we enter our final chapter is:

Direct Vs Regular Plan.

When investing in mutual funds, one of the most common confusions people face is whether to choose a Direct Plan or a Regular Plan. While both invest in the same mutual fund scheme and are managed by the same fund house, the difference lies in how you invest and who guides you. In a Direct Plan, you invest directly with the AMC (Asset Management Company) without involving an intermediary or distributor. Because there's no middleman, the expense ratio is slightly lower, which means the returns appear higher in the long run. However, in a Direct Plan, you are entirely on your own — from selecting the right fund to monitoring performance, rebalancing, making switches, planning withdrawals, and handling SEBI/AMFI regulatory changes. There's no professional guiding your decisions, which can be risky if you're not deeply knowledgeable about markets, asset allocation, taxation rules, or portfolio strategy.

A Regular Plan, on the other hand, is facilitated through a SEBI-registered Mutual Fund Distributor (MFD) or advisor. Here, the expense ratio is slightly higher because a part of it goes as commission to the distributor for their services. This often leads investors to think they are "losing returns" by paying this commission — but in reality, a good distributor adds value far beyond that cost. An experienced MFD helps you in choosing the right funds, setting up the right asset allocation, reviewing your portfolio periodically, suggesting timely switches, ensuring you remain disciplined during volatile markets, and structuring withdrawals like SWP in a tax-efficient way. They also take care of documentation, nomination updates, and regulatory changes so you don't have to track every detail yourself. Many investors in Direct Plans tend to make emotional decisions during market highs and lows, leading to wrong timing and lower actual returns than what the fund delivers on paper. In comparison, investors in Regular Plans benefit from consistent handholding, staying invested for the long term, and avoiding costly mistakes. This behavioural advantage often outweighs the small difference in expense ratio, making the Regular Plan worth every rupee for those who value guidance, discipline, and peace of mind in their wealth-building journey.

10

Final Words – Where Do You Begin?

Because Knowledge Without Action is Useless

We've come a long way.

From understanding why most people struggle financially…

To discovering the power of SIPs, SWPs, Mutual Funds, and the need of Financial Planning…

To imagining a life of freedom, dignity, and generational wealth.

But let's ask the one question that matters most now:

What will you do next?

You Don't Need to Know Everything.

You Just Need to Begin.

Don't wait until:

- You earn more
- The market is "perfect"
- You finish 5 more books
- Someone else tells you it's time

The time is **NOW**.

Not tomorrow. Not next year. Not "someday."

Your Action Plan (Start Today):

1. Set one clear financial goal

– Retirement corpus? Kids' education? Early freedom?

2. Start your first SIP

– Even if it's ₹2000/month. Get the habit started.

3. Talk to a financial advisor

– Not because you're weak — but because you're serious.

4. Create your emergency fund

– Start with 3 months of expenses in a liquid fund or savings.

5. Review your life insurance and health insurance

– Protect first, then grow.

6. Automate. Stay consistent. Trust the process.

A Personal Note from Me to You

You don't need to be a financial genius.

You don't need to be rich to begin.

You only need two things:

- A reason (your "why")
- A rhythm (your monthly SIPs)

I've seen teachers, drivers, small shopkeepers, and government staff turn their lives around — not by magic, but by discipline.

If they can, so can you.

Your Wealth Journey Starts Here ...

Final Thoughts

Let this book not just be a source of knowledge...

Let it be the spark that changed your financial destiny.

And if this helped you — pass it on.

Help others break free from the salary trap.

Help your children start early.

Help your family build better habits.

You now have the tools.

Use them. Share them.

Build wealth. Live free. Leave a legacy.

If there's one final thing I want you to take away from this book, it's that building wealth is not about chasing quick returns — it's about having a clear plan, staying disciplined, and making informed decisions year after year. That's exactly what I help my clients do at ACE INVESTMENTS. Whether it's designing the perfect SIP strategy, creating an SWP that gives you a lifetime income, or structuring your portfolio to beat inflation and secure your family's future, my mission is to guide you every step of the way. With years of experience, market knowledge, and a genuine passion for financial education, I'm here to ensure you don't just invest, but invest right. So, when you're ready to turn your goals into reality, let's connect — and start building the financial freedom you deserve.

"You can work for money your whole life.

Or… you can learn how to make money work for you."

Choose wisely.

— Nihal Kashinath Kirnalli

AMFI Registered Mutual Fund Distributor

ACE INVESTMENTS | 7385 505090 | investwithnihal@gmail.com

Socials:

1. www.instagram.com/InvestWithNihal_Mutualfunds
2. www.facebook.com/InvestWithNihal
3. www.youtube.com/@InvestWithNihal
4. www.linkedin.com/in/nihalkirnalli/

www.ingramcontent.com/pod-product-compliance
Lightning Source LLC
LaVergne TN
LVHW090429210926
848480LV00002B/745